This Gift Log Belongs To:

_____

_____

_____

 Gift Log

Date	Gift	Thank You Sent
		♥
From		
Address		
Date	Gift	Thank You Sent
		♥
From		
Address		
Date	Gift	Thank You Sent
		♥
From		
Address		
Date	Gift	Thank You Sent
		♥
From		
Address		

 Gift Log

Date	Gift	Thank You Sent
		♥
From		
Address		
Date	Gift	Thank You Sent
		♥
From		
Address		
Date	Gift	Thank You Sent
		♥
From		
Address		
Date	Gift	Thank You Sent
		♥
From		
Address		

 Gift Log

Date	Gift	Thank You Sent
From		
Address		

Date	Gift	Thank You Sent
From		
Address		

Date	Gift	Thank You Sent
From		
Address		

Date	Gift	Thank You Sent
From		
Address		

 Gift Log

Date	Gift	Thank You Sent
		♥
From		
Address		
Date	Gift	Thank You Sent
		♥
From		
Address		
Date	Gift	Thank You Sent
		♥
From		
Address		
Date	Gift	Thank You Sent
		♥
From		
Address		

 Gift Log

Date	Gift	Thank You Sent

From		
Address		
Date	Gift	Thank You Sent
From		
Address		
Date	Gift	Thank You Sent
From		
Address		
Date	Gift	Thank You Sent
From		
Address		

Gift Log

Date	Gift	Thank You Sent
		♥
From		
Address		
Date	Gift	Thank You Sent
		♥
From		
Address		
Date	Gift	Thank You Sent
		♥
From		
Address		
Date	Gift	Thank You Sent
		♥
From		
Address		

 Gift Log

Date	Gift	Thank You Sent
		♥
From		
Address		
Date	Gift	Thank You Sent
		♥
From		
Address		
Date	Gift	Thank You Sent
		♥
From		
Address		
Date	Gift	Thank You Sent
		♥
From		
Address		

 Gift Log

Date	Gift	Thank You Sent
		♥
From		
Address		
Date	Gift	Thank You Sent
		♥
From		
Address		
Date	Gift	Thank You Sent
		♥
From		
Address		
Date	Gift	Thank You Sent
		♥
From		
Address		

 Gift Log

Date	Gift	Thank You Sent
		♥
From		
Address		
Date	Gift	Thank You Sent
		♥
From		
Address		
Date	Gift	Thank You Sent
		♥
From		
Address		
Date	Gift	Thank You Sent
		♥
From		
Address		

Gift Log

Date	Gift	Thank You Sent
		♥
From		
Address		
Date	Gift	Thank You Sent
		♥
From		
Address		
Date	Gift	Thank You Sent
		♥
From		
Address		
Date	Gift	Thank You Sent
		♥
From		
Address		

 Gift Log

Date	Gift	Thank You Sent

From		
Address		

Date	Gift	Thank You Sent
From		
Address		

Date	Gift	Thank You Sent
From		
Address		

Date	Gift	Thank You Sent
From		
Address		

 Gift Log

Date	Gift	Thank You Sent
		♥
From		
Address		
Date	Gift	Thank You Sent
		♥
From		
Address		
Date	Gift	Thank You Sent
		♥
From		
Address		
Date	Gift	Thank You Sent
		♥
From		
Address		

♥ Gift Log ♥

Date	Gift	Thank You Sent
		♥
From		
Address		
Date	Gift	Thank You Sent
		♥
From		
Address		
Date	Gift	Thank You Sent
		♥
From		
Address		
Date	Gift	Thank You Sent
		♥
From		
Address		

Gift Log

Date	Gift	Thank You Sent
		♥
From		
Address		

Date	Gift	Thank You Sent
		♥
From		
Address		

Date	Gift	Thank You Sent
		♥
From		
Address		

Date	Gift	Thank You Sent
		♥
From		
Address		

Gift Log

Date	Gift	Thank You Sent
		♥
From		
Address		
Date	Gift	Thank You Sent
		♥
From		
Address		
Date	Gift	Thank You Sent
		♥
From		
Address		
Date	Gift	Thank You Sent
		♥
From		
Address		

Gift Log

Date	Gift	Thank You Sent
From		
Address		
Date	Gift	Thank You Sent
From		
Address		
Date	Gift	Thank You Sent
From		
Address		
Date	Gift	Thank You Sent
From		
Address		

♥ Gift Log ♥

Date	Gift	Thank You Sent
		♥
From		
Address		
Date	Gift	Thank You Sent
		♥
From		
Address		
Date	Gift	Thank You Sent
		♥
From		
Address		
Date	Gift	Thank You Sent
		♥
From		
Address		

Gift Log

Date	Gift	Thank You Sent
		♥
From		
Address		
Date	Gift	Thank You Sent
		♥
From		
Address		
Date	Gift	Thank You Sent
		♥
From		
Address		
Date	Gift	Thank You Sent
		♥
From		
Address		

♥ Gift Log ♥

Date	Gift	Thank You Sent
		♥
From		
Address		
Date	Gift	Thank You Sent
		♥
From		
Address		
Date	Gift	Thank You Sent
		♥
From		
Address		
Date	Gift	Thank You Sent
		♥
From		
Address		

 Gift Log

Date	Gift	Thank You Sent
		♥
From		
Address		

Date	Gift	Thank You Sent
		♥
From		
Address		

Date	Gift	Thank You Sent
		♥
From		
Address		

Date	Gift	Thank You Sent
		♥
From		
Address		

 Gift Log

Date	Gift	Thank You Sent
		♥
From		
Address		

Date	Gift	Thank You Sent
		♥
From		
Address		

Date	Gift	Thank You Sent
		♥
From		
Address		

Date	Gift	Thank You Sent
		♥
From		
Address		

 Gift Log

Date	Gift	Thank You Sent
		♥
From		
Address		
Date	Gift	Thank You Sent
		♥
From		
Address		
Date	Gift	Thank You Sent
		♥
From		
Address		
Date	Gift	Thank You Sent
		♥
From		
Address		

 Gift Log

Date	Gift	Thank You Sent
		♥
From		
Address		

Date	Gift	Thank You Sent
		♥
From		
Address		

Date	Gift	Thank You Sent
		♥
From		
Address		

Date	Gift	Thank You Sent
		♥
From		
Address		

 Gift Log

Date	Gift	Thank You Sent
		♥
From		
Address		
Date	Gift	Thank You Sent
		♥
From		
Address		
Date	Gift	Thank You Sent
		♥
From		
Address		
Date	Gift	Thank You Sent
		♥
From		
Address		

 Gift Log

Date	Gift	Thank You Sent
		♥
From		
Address		

Date	Gift	Thank You Sent
		♥
From		
Address		

Date	Gift	Thank You Sent
		♥
From		
Address		

Date	Gift	Thank You Sent
		♥
From		
Address		

Gift Log

Date	Gift	Thank You Sent
		♥
From		
Address		
Date	Gift	Thank You Sent
		♥
From		
Address		
Date	Gift	Thank You Sent
		♥
From		
Address		
Date	Gift	Thank You Sent
		♥
From		
Address		

♥ Gift Log ♥

Date	Gift	Thank You Sent
		♥
From		
Address		

Date	Gift	Thank You Sent
		♥
From		
Address		

Date	Gift	Thank You Sent
		♥
From		
Address		

Date	Gift	Thank You Sent
		♥
From		
Address		

 Gift Log

Date	Gift	Thank You Sent
		♥
From		
Address		

Date	Gift	Thank You Sent
		♥
From		
Address		

Date	Gift	Thank You Sent
		♥
From		
Address		

Date	Gift	Thank You Sent
		♥
From		
Address		

♥ Gift Log ♥

Date	Gift	Thank You Sent
		♥
From		
Address		
Date	Gift	Thank You Sent
		♥
From		
Address		
Date	Gift	Thank You Sent
		♥
From		
Address		
Date	Gift	Thank You Sent
		♥
From		
Address		

 Gift Log

Date	Gift	Thank You Sent
		♥
From		
Address		

Date	Gift	Thank You Sent
		♥
From		
Address		

Date	Gift	Thank You Sent
		♥
From		
Address		

Date	Gift	Thank You Sent
		♥
From		
Address		

♡ Gift Log ♡

Date	Gift	Thank You Sent
		♡
From		
Address		
Date	Gift	Thank You Sent
		♡
From		
Address		
Date	Gift	Thank You Sent
		♡
From		
Address		
Date	Gift	Thank You Sent
		♡
From		
Address		

 Gift Log

Date	Gift	Thank You Sent
		♥
From		
Address		
Date	Gift	Thank You Sent
		♥
From		
Address		
Date	Gift	Thank You Sent
		♥
From		
Address		
Date	Gift	Thank You Sent
		♥
From		
Address		

♥ Gift Log ♥

Date	Gift	Thank You Sent
		♥
From		
Address		
Date	Gift	Thank You Sent
		♥
From		
Address		
Date	Gift	Thank You Sent
		♥
From		
Address		
Date	Gift	Thank You Sent
		♥
From		
Address		

 Gift Log

Date	Gift	Thank You Sent
		♥
From		
Address		

Date	Gift	Thank You Sent
		♥
From		
Address		

Date	Gift	Thank You Sent
		♥
From		
Address		

Date	Gift	Thank You Sent
		♥
From		
Address		

 Gift Log

Date	Gift	Thank You Sent
		♥
From		
Address		
Date	Gift	Thank You Sent
		♥
From		
Address		
Date	Gift	Thank You Sent
		♥
From		
Address		
Date	Gift	Thank You Sent
		♥
From		
Address		

 Gift Log

Date	Gift	Thank You Sent
		♥
From		
Address		

Date	Gift	Thank You Sent
		♥
From		
Address		

Date	Gift	Thank You Sent
		♥
From		
Address		

Date	Gift	Thank You Sent
		♥
From		
Address		

 Gift Log

Date	Gift	Thank You Sent
		♥
From		
Address		
Date	Gift	Thank You Sent
		♥
From		
Address		
Date	Gift	Thank You Sent
		♥
From		
Address		
Date	Gift	Thank You Sent
		♥
From		
Address		

Gift Log

Date	Gift	Thank You Sent
		♥
From		
Address		
Date	Gift	Thank You Sent
		♥
From		
Address		
Date	Gift	Thank You Sent
		♥
From		
Address		
Date	Gift	Thank You Sent
		♥
From		
Address		

 Gift Log

Date	Gift	Thank You Sent
		♥
From		
Address		

Date	Gift	Thank You Sent
		♥
From		
Address		

Date	Gift	Thank You Sent
		♥
From		
Address		

Date	Gift	Thank You Sent
		♥
From		
Address		

Gift Log

Date	Gift	Thank You Sent
		♥
From		
Address		

Date	Gift	Thank You Sent
		♥
From		
Address		

Date	Gift	Thank You Sent
		♥
From		
Address		

Date	Gift	Thank You Sent
		♥
From		
Address		

Gift Log

Date	Gift	Thank You Sent

From		
Address		
Date	Gift	Thank You Sent
From		
Address		
Date	Gift	Thank You Sent
From		
Address		
Date	Gift	Thank You Sent
From		
Address		

Gift Log

Date	Gift	Thank You Sent
		♥
From		
Address		
Date	Gift	Thank You Sent
		♥
From		
Address		
Date	Gift	Thank You Sent
		♥
From		
Address		
Date	Gift	Thank You Sent
		♥
From		
Address		

 Gift Log

Date	Gift	Thank You Sent
		♥
From		
Address		
Date	Gift	Thank You Sent
		♥
From		
Address		
Date	Gift	Thank You Sent
		♥
From		
Address		
Date	Gift	Thank You Sent
		♥
From		
Address		

 Gift Log

Date	Gift	Thank You Sent
		♥
From		
Address		
Date	Gift	Thank You Sent
		♥
From		
Address		
Date	Gift	Thank You Sent
		♥
From		
Address		
Date	Gift	Thank You Sent
		♥
From		
Address		

 Gift Log

Date	Gift	Thank You Sent
		♥
From		
Address		
Date	Gift	Thank You Sent
		♥
From		
Address		
Date	Gift	Thank You Sent
		♥
From		
Address		
Date	Gift	Thank You Sent
		♥
From		
Address		

 Gift Log

Date	Gift	Thank You Sent
		♥
From		
Address		

Date	Gift	Thank You Sent
		♥
From		
Address		

Date	Gift	Thank You Sent
		♥
From		
Address		

Date	Gift	Thank You Sent
		♥
From		
Address		

 Gift Log

Date	Gift	Thank You Sent

From		
Address		
Date	Gift	Thank You Sent
From		
Address		
Date	Gift	Thank You Sent
From		
Address		
Date	Gift	Thank You Sent
From		
Address		

Made in United States
Orlando, FL
04 April 2025

60160060R00031